Roy Goes Camping

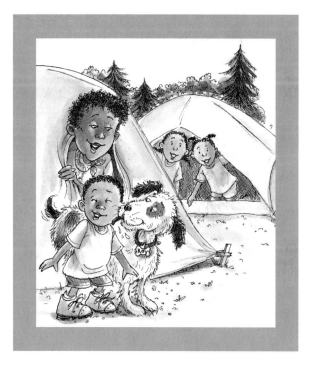

by Betsy Franco
illustrated by Amy Wummer

Scott Foresman

Editorial Offices: Glenview, Illinois • New York, New York
Sales Offices: Reading, Massachusetts • Duluth, Georgia
Glenview, Illinois • Carrollton, Texas • Menlo Park, California

"School starts in three days.
Let's go camping!" said Mom.
"Can Roy come?" asked Kim.
"Yes," said Mom.

Everyone packed the car.
Troy got his toys. Kim got
the foil and oil. Joy got the
sleeping bags.

It was getting late. They were
lost. Joy found a map. She
pointed to the campground.

"There's one spot left," said Kim.
"The spot isn't very big. But we'll
fit. It will not spoil our trip!"

They made a campfire. Roy
started digging in the soil.
Kim yelled, "Move, Roy,
move! You can't spoil our trip!"

Troy wouldn't sleep.

"Noise is fine," Mom said.

"There's always noise. Noise will
not spoil our trip!"

In the morning, they made
a fire. They boiled eggs. They
made toast on the foil.

"The boiled eggs are fine. The toast is burned," said Joy. "But the toast isn't that bad. It will not spoil our trip!"

Kim said, "Roy enjoys the
toast! He enjoys the eggs too!
Good boy, Roy."

"We don't have raincoats,"
said Mom. "But rain will not
spoil our trip!"

Then it was time to go. Joy
pointed to a rainbow.
    She shouted, "We had fun!
Not one thing spoiled our trip!"

Phonics for Families: This book gives your child practice in reading words with the letters *oy* and *oi*, as in *boy* and *spoil*; words with more than one syllable, such as *campfire* and *isn't*; and the high-frequency words *boy, school, open, move,* and *always.* Have your child read the book with you. Then ask your child to find words that rhyme with *boy* (*Roy, Troy, Joy*) and *boil* (*foil, oil, spoil, soil*).

Phonics Skill: Vowel diphthongs *oi, oy;* Multisyllabic words (compounds, contractions); Inflected endings

High-Frequency Words: *boy, school, open, move, always*